William H(

# Farmers Markets: A Guide to Small

# Scale Business and Entrepreneurship

## William Hood English

William Hood English

ISBN: 0692512985

ISBN-13: 978-0-692-51298-2

**Farmers Market: A Guide to Small Scale Business and Entrepreneurship** By William H. English

**Editing by crowd sourced team:** Janet Law, Jerry Van Leuven, Benson Smith, Paul Vial, Reme Pullicar, Gregg Fisher, Lisa Schuneman, Melissa Nodzu, Frances English, David Turner

**ISBN-13:** 978-0-692-51298-2
**ISBN:10:** 0-692-51298-5

**Printed** in the United States of America

**Published by**: Blue Creek Publishing. (www.bluecreekpublishing.com)

# DEDICATION AND ACKNOWLEDGEMENT

I have always been impressed by those brave souls who implement an idea for a business or want to work for themselves – even in a small way. Hence, I have written this guide for current and potential vendors at Farmers Markets. Therefore, it is dedicated to you the reader, who is or wants to be a small scale entrepreneur. Good luck to you. I trust this guide will help you achieve success in your business endeavors.

I would also like to dedicate this book to all those Farmers Market vendors who took the time to answer my questionnaires as well as the numerous follow up questions and agreed to be interviewed. Thanks, I really appreciate your input.

## BILL ENGLISH

# TABLE OF CONTENTS

## SECTION 4:  Small Scale Entrepreneurship

# SECTION 1:

# Farmers Markets:

# A Business Opportunity for You?

# TOPIC 1

# FORWARD AND INTRODUCTION TO FARMERS MARKETS

Farmers Markets are probably some of the earliest examples of man's entrepreneurial spirit which continues into today's modern societies across most countries of the Earth. Gathering places, usually urban centers small and large, were established where farmers could bring their produce, food animals etc. to town to sell their products to hungry urban dwellers. Here farmers found customers with cash and customers found fresh food items at reasonable prices.

Today, these same conditions exist, but the product alignments of modern Farmers Markets have significantly increased. Now in addition to fresh produce, eggs, meats, and dairy products, you will find art, jewelry, pastries, baked goods, craft goods, clothes, sewing goods, artisan cheeses, etc.

I can remember as a young boy growing up in southeastern Michigan, the thoughts I had about running my own business. This may have been fostered in some degree by having a paper route delivering the Detroit Times newspaper. However, when I was in college, the idea of any business ownership took a back seat to working for one of the "Big Three" automotive companies. It was a great career with many challenges and rewards. Eventually, I left the big corporate organization and joined a small automotive related sales agency, eventually buying the company. Since that time, I have owned several different companies.

However, upon reflection, I now wish I had gotten my feet wet sooner, with the challenges and rewards of business ownership. I would have learned great lessons, some of which might have saved me from making financial mistakes in my later years. I also might have learned some lessons that could have expanded my opportunities and knowledge, greatly benefiting me.

Additionally, I could have used those early business opportunities to supplement my income.

For the entrepreneur of any age or stage of life, there are fundamental questions that have to be asked in order to maximize one's potential for success and minimize one's financial investment. Some of those questions might be:

• What kind of business do I start? Your skills, knowledge, interests, experience, hobbies, etc., will help answer this question.

• Where do I find customers?

• How do I market to those customers?

• How do I minimize my investment and maximize my profits?

• Where do I find my products, or do I make quality products myself?

• How do I learn from successful entrepreneurs who have made the plunge into running a small (maybe tiny) business?

• What kind of part-time, or full-time fun business can I operate to minimize my financial risks and enjoy a financial reward?

There are many answers to the above individual questions. But in my opinion, Farmers Markets answers almost all the above questions in a positive manner.

At a Farmers Market, with minimal financial investment, but lots of work, planning and implementation, you can test your ideas, products, skills, etc., to establish and operate a functional part-time business. Here, lots of potential customers will walk past your business front, stop and look, taste, and maybe buy. This is a place where you can talk face to face with your customer, answer and ask questions, have fun and make some money.

There are very few other business environments where you will have these kinds of business opportunities in such abundance. One insightful Farmers Market vendor shared with me the following statement: "Farmers Markets are one of the only places where lots of people come with empty bags/baskets expecting to fill them and full wallets/purses ready to spend."

This narrative will concentrate on the opportunities associated with the non-agricultural aspects of operating an independent, innovative, part-time or full-time Farmers Market business for your personal and financial growth and training. Included will be stories and first person accounts and quotes of those who took the opportunity to step into the market square and experience success.

Farmers Markets are a growth industry. See the "National Count of Farmers Markets Directory Listing" bar graph below. In the last 10 years (2006 – 2016), the number of Farmers Markets across the USA has increased by 98% and 2.3% growth between 2015 and 2016.. This amazing growth is fueled by individuals who have embraced the concepts of entrepreneurship as they started their own Farmers Market businesses. If there were only an average of 20 vendor booths at each market, it represents almost 175,000 vendor booths in operation every week throughout the summer/fall. These booths are mostly operated by small scale, part time entrepreneurs who have accepted the challenges and rewards of owning and operating their own businesses. **You could be among them!**

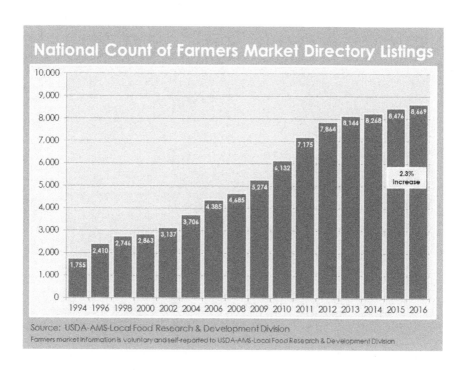

Farmers Markets can be big business. For example, the Farmers Market in Boise Idaho has over 150 vendors, which contributes over $4,000,000 annually to the Boise economy. Each Saturday, between 12,000 and 15,000 people attend the Boise Farmers Market.

This book is intended to be a quick read, with basic information that can be easily understood and implemented to facilitate the readers' success in operating a Farmers Market booth. For existing Farmers Market vendors, you too will find many nuggets of value within these pages, which will help you in your business. Also included is information regarding true entrepreneurship for those who choose to expand their business within the Farmers Market venue or reach out to other retail/wholesale venues.

# TOPIC 2

# WHY FARMERS MARKETS?

I hope by the time you have read this book, you will agree with me that Farmers Markets are the perfect business for the person who wants:

- A part-time business. Most of the time it will be a part-time, warm weather business.

- A business with limited operating hours and days.

- Some flexibility in your work schedule – you can take a day off.

- A business that can grow.

- A small business that can lead to bigger things.

- A steady stream of potential customers willing to buy.

- No advertising expense.

- A mostly cash business.

- To be your own boss.

- Small capital investment.

- Low rent for your booth, no long term lease.

- Low overhead.

- A business that is simple to change and in which it is easy to see results.
- A business that provides the opportunity to learn about business and put that knowledge into practice.
- To see your business ideas come to fruition.
- See if you are really cut out to own and operate a business.
- An opportunity to make some extra income.
- To involve your family in the business.
- Other businesses nearby with owners who are willing to help you succeed.
- A business in which failure won't bankrupt you.
- An enjoyable environment in which you can work.
- A business which allows you to work outside in the fresh air.
- An opportunity to meet and talk with (mostly) happy people.

The attributes listed above will go a long way toward helping the ambitious, small scale entrepreneur enhance their chances of success and hopefully, help the owner to be happy.


## Kim and Mark

Kim and Mark are great examples of "Why Farmers Markets". They lived in Wisconsin, known as America's Dairyland because it is one of America's leading dairy producers. Kim and Mark did not grow up in farming families, but describe themselves as cheese enthusiasts, like most Wisconsinites. Mark's previous business did connect him to many of Wisconsin's dairies, big and small.

They loved traveling to the western states and decided to move west. However, when they got west they did not have a job. When their new friends found out they were from Wisconsin, they often asked about cheese.

Kim and Mark liked to eat cheese curds but they found it difficult to find cheese curds in their area. They decided if they liked cheese curds, but couldn't find the curds, maybe westerners would also like them and be willing to buy them. Kim and Mark decided to sell cheese curds. They did some online searches and found some prospective cheese curd suppliers in their home state of Wisconsin. After some phone and personal contact, they settled on a small artesian cheese maker.

Now they had to sell the cheese curds. Their supplier was not large enough to supply the volumes required in a retail outlet and Kim and Mark did not want to market wholesale. Therefore, without any previous Farmers Market experience, one year ago they decided to set up a booth at a Farmers Market. The curds sold. Now Kim and Mark have booths at seven Farmers Markets spread over five days a week.

Farmers Markets provided Kim and Mark an opportunity to develop a profitable business, to meet and talk to their happy customers and thoroughly enjoy their business venture.

## Stacy

Stacy liked to make chocolate candy and through her experiments and expertise, she has developed some unique and delicious chocolate candies. She also wanted to have a small business as her mother had done with cakes. However, Stacy did not want the demands, expense and risk of opening a brick and mortar retail storefront to sell her yummy, melt in your mouth chocolate creations. She decided Farmers Markets presented the best opportunity for success. So with a little trepidation and much excitement, she and her business partner decided they would open a Farmers Market booth. Their customers agreed their chocolate creations were delicious. The business grew. They now operate up to eight Farmers Market booths per week.

They soon found the bulk of their business was for "made to order' chocolates. But those orders were generated at their Farmers Market booths.

Since they ship a delicate commodity that can melt, they wanted to ensure that that did not happen in transit. So they did some test shipments using cooler packs, to friends on the other side of the country to ensure the chocolate arrived fresh and in good condition. Their friends were more than happy to be on the receiving end of the shipping tests.

## QUESTION:

**Which of the above attributes (and others you may have thought of) appeal to you?**

_____

_____

_____

# TOPIC 3

# WHAT IS FOR SALE AT FARMERS MARKETS?

When you look at all the things people sell at Farmers Markets, they can be grouped into four categories:

1.  Farm Produce, Plants, Seedlings, Meats, etc

2.  Processed / Prepared Foods

3.  Arts and Crafts

4.  Other Products

As you review the following lists, you will find they are rife with opportunities for the small scale entrepreneur. The lists are not intended to be all inclusive, but to provide you with an awareness of products that can be sold at Farmers Markets. Some items are shown on more than one list.

Hopefully these lists will spark an interest or help bring to mind products you could sell at your booth. Also, in your daily activities, you might come across a product that might sell well at a Farmers Market or be able to be sold as an artesan or gourmet product. For example, my wife and I recently had lunch at a new restaurant which served a unique Lemon Basil salad dressing, which my wife loved. Could that be sold at a Farmers Market or sold nationally? Do you have fond memories of some food that your Mother or Grandmother served? Can you replicate it and sell it at your Farmers Market booth?

One of the most unique items I have seen sold at a Farmers Market, was work gloves. That was all the vendor sold. There must have been fifteen or more varieties of work gloves (leather and cloth – mostly leather) stacked on three tables. The vendor has been successfully selling only work gloves at Farmers Markets for many years.

I also saw a Farmers Market vendor who sold dog scarves and leashes, harnesses, collars, etc. He had his booth displayed with toy dogs wearing his harnesses, collars, etc. and he also had several nice, colorful displays of his various products. He attracted a nice crowd of people.

The reason I point out these two items is to show how a product one would think is too specialized  can be successfully sold at a Farmers Market.

## QUESTION:

**What do you plan to sell at your Farmers Market?**

_____

_____

_____

## FARM PRODUCTS FOR SALE AT FARMERS MARKETS

Butter

Cheeses of all kinds

Cider

Flowers, Fresh Cut

Fruits: Apples, Peaches, Pears, Nuts, Corn etc.

Herbs, fresh and dried

Lavender

Maple Syrup

Meats, all kinds of cuts

Meats: organic and/or grass fed

Meats: beef, pork, goat, lamb

Mushroom Growing Kits

Mushrooms

Nursery Bedding Supplies

Peppers

Pigeon, frozen

Plants

Potatoes: white and sweet

Poultry

Produce of all kinds

Pumpkins and Gourds

Rabbits, frozen

Rosehips

Sausages of all kinds

Seedlings

Squash of all kinds

## FOOD ITEMS FOR SALE AT FARMERS MARKETS

Apple butter

Baba ghanoujj

Baked goods, gluten free

Bakery Items of all kinds

Baklava

BBQ sauces

Biscotti: regular, vegan, gluten free

Bleu cheese

Bloody Mary Mixes (rub, Italian, drinks)

Bread puddings, various flavors

Breadings, gourmet

Brownies

Burritos

Cakes of all kinds

Caramel, various flavors

Cashew brittle

Casseroles

Catering services

Cheese curds, cheddar, etc

Cheese, cheddar

Cheese, cream

Cheese, curds

Cheese, flavored

Cheese, gouda

Chewy caramels

Chicken pot pies

Chili, frozen and fresh

Chilies, green and dried

Chipotle

Chocolate truffles

Chocolates, handmade artisan

Chutney, sweet or hot, various flavors

Coffees, select artisan and regular

Cookies of all kinds

Cotton candy

Cracklins

Crepes cooked to order

Croissants

Cupcakes

Dipping sauces and mixes

Donuts, fried fresh

Dried fruit

Energy bars

Fish, smoked

Flat breads

Flours, gluten free

Flowers, dried and fresh

French baguettes

French fries

Fresh rolls

Frozen entrees,

Frozen soups

Fruit leathers

Fudges of all kinds

Garlic butter

Garlics

Gelato from vintage ice cream truck

Gingerbread

Goat cheeses of all flavors and mixes

Goat milk

Granolas of all types

Grape leaves – stuffed

Heirloom tomatoes and vegetables

Herbs

Hickory syrup

Honey, whipped, regular, stick, clover, orange, etc.

Horseradish

Hot dogs, cheese dogs, chili dogs, etc

Hummus

Infused cooking and dipping oils

Jalapeno pepper jellies

Jambalayas

Jams, jellies, preserves and pastels

Jerky: beef, bison, elk, etc

Juices of all kinds

Lard, homemade

Lasagna, take and bake

Lemonade

Marmalades

Marshmallow Krispies with various additives/flavors

Marshmallows, big and fluffy

Meat pies

Meats, kosher

Meats, organic

Mud bars

Nachos

Olive oils and vinegars

Organic herbs and oils

Pasties

Peanut brittle, hand crafted

Pecan candy

Pepper concoctions

Pepper spreads

Pestos, various flavors

Pickles of all kinds

Pierogies

Pies, of all kinds

Pies, small single serving

Pies, sweet potato

Pita breads

Popcorn, balls, caramel, flavored

Pralines

Papusas

Quesadilla

Quiches, regular and vegetarian

Raw chocolate

Root beer, home made

Rosehips

Salad dressings of all kinds

Salad dressings, regional and special

Salsas, red and green, etc

Salted caramel sauce

Sauces and rubs

Sausages and wurst, gourmet

Savana Bars

Scones

Seafoods, vacuum packed

Seasoning salts

Seasonings, custom

Seeds, flower

Shortbreads

Snow cones

Soul foods

Soups of various kinds

Spices

Stroopwafel cookies

Sweet breads

Syrups, maple etc

Taco shells

Tacos

Tapenades

Tarts

Toffee, gourmet

Tamales, hot or frozen

Tortillas

Vanilla, hand crafted

Wedges

Wheat grass and shoots

Wines, handcrafted and bottled

Wisecakes

Whoopie pies

## ARTS AND CRAFTS ITEMS FOR SALE AT FARMERS MARKETS.

Apiary products

Aprons of all kinds

Art glass, flat bottles etc.

Baby baskets

Bags and purses

Bows and ribbons

Brooches and other metal jewelry

Candles: Wax and Soy and Sentsy ™

Children's books by author

Clothing – dresses, etc

Crocheted items

Deodorants

Dog biscuits, gourmet

Dried flower arrangements

Earrings of all kinds

Electronic cases, hand crafted

Essential oils and scents

Fresh cut flower arrangements

Fruit baskets

Garden art items

Greeting cards

Guitars and ukuleles, custom built

Hammocks: hand crafted, woven

Hat bands

Headbands, hairclips, etc.

Jewelry, originals

Jewelry, recrafted

Jewelry, recycled

Jewelry, wooden

Knitted hats, mittens, scarfs

Leather belts, purses, wallets, etc.

Leather tooled purses, bags, wallets, and holsters

Lip balms

Lotions

Matted and framed photos

Metal figures, designs, sundials, etc.

Original fashions

Painted gourds and pumpkins

Paintings of all kinds and media

Paintings, oils

Paintings, pastels

Paintings, watercolor

Photography: landscapes, animals, etc.

Placards, funny, artistic

Pottery of all kinds

Quilted table runners

Sachets and eye pillows

Sand-cast leaf garden art

Shaving brushes

Shawls

Soaps, fizzes, etc., hand crafted

Stained glass

Stone picture frames

Textile accessories

Three dimensional artwork

Tie-dyed scarves, shirts, etc.

Totes

Wooden cutting blocks

Wooden spoons, ladles, forks, etc.

Wooden toys

Wooden utensils from your trees, custom made

Woven rugs

Wreaths


## **OTHER ITEMS FOR SALE AT FARMERS MARKETS**

Alpaca products

Antiques

Apiary products

Apothecary items

Baby and toddler enriching classes

Balloon art

Beeswax candles

Bikes, trail and mountain

Birdhouse kits, build yourself

Birdhouses and feeders

Books, children's by author

Canes and staffs

Catnip

Chiropractic services

Credit Union providers

Dog treats and food

Doll clothes

Earthworm growing kits

Elixirs

Essential Oils

Face painting

Feathers

Fire pits, metal

Fitness Clubs

Furniture design and custom built

Furniture repair and/or refurbish

Gloves, work gloves of all kinds

Hair accessories, bows, ribbons, etc

Hammocks

Hand crafted wooden ink pens

Handyman services

Home repair and remodeling

Homestead supply products

Iron work

Lavender sachets and eye pillows

Leather goods (purses, wallets, belts, etc)

Minerals, healthy

Minerals, raw

Mushroom growing kits

Performers, singing, playing instruments

Pet foods

Pet leashes and harnesses

Pet treats

Photography services

Remedies

Replacement windows

Salves

Sharpening services

Signs and home décor

Songbird supplies, blended seeds

Spa items

Tinctures

Tonics

T-Shirts, various

Tutoring services

Walking sticks

# SECTION 2:

# Setting Up Your Business

# TOPIC 4

# REGISTER YOUR BUSINESS AND PURCHASE INSURANCE

Business ownership is a great experience, full of challenges and rewards. Many people think when they have their own business, they are their own boss. But when the hard facts of reality settle in, owners find they have many bosses. Each of their customers becomes a boss – someone to please and meet their expectations. However, even with all these bosses, as the owner you still set your hours and decide when you are going to work. And of course, you reap the rewards (financial and personal) of implementing your ideas, taking measured risks, investing your money and time.

**Register Your Business**: But before you can sell your wares, you need to register your business. If you are going to be selling food items, there will probably be additional requirements (see commercial or commissary kitchens section). The registration process can be relatively easy. Check with your state, county and city official websites for information. The local Farmers Market management team will usually be able to help you accomplish this and they might have a hand-out that lists all the pertinent websites, etc. Usually there will also be phone contact information listed on the website for personal assistance. Call them, that is why they are listed. The requirements are going to be different for each location you are going to set up your business. Therefore, I cannot list those requirements in this book. The key to avoiding problems and surprises is to be compliant with the requirements.

**Insurance:** Unfortunately, we live in a very litigious society where we are too quick to run to our attorney and discuss suing the other party. If we are in business, we cannot afford to be without insurance to provide some protection against law suits etc. Additionally, some states will require business owners to carry certain kinds of insurance for the business. Check the requirements for your state, then discuss the policies and prices available with a trusted insurance agent. You will at a minimum need liability insurance. Some states will also require you to carry workman's compensation insurance. Again, check with your insurance agent. The Farmers Market might also require you to carry certain kinds of insurance in order to rent a booth at their market. Check the requirements.

## COMMENTS / QUESTIONS:

**List the websites you will need to contact to take care of the registration of your company (also list the phone number of the**

**person you talked to, if applicable).**

_____

_____

_____

_____

_____

**What insurance do you need?**

_____

_____

_____

| Company | Agent | Phone Number | Amount |
|---------|-------|--------------|--------|
| | | | |
| | | | |
| | | | |

# TOPIC 5

# STARTING OR MODIFYING YOUR FARMERS MARKET BUSINESS

When is a good time to start or modify your Farmers Market business? In probably 90% of the time, the answer is now! I firmly believe in planning, but there comes a time when you have to put that plan into action. You cannot keep waiting for the economy to "get right". Your effective business plan should be based on the current economy. Being thoroughly prepared with a great plan, product, and packaging is probably more important than the economy.

The trick to success is to have a good business plan (and a good product people will buy). Do some research. What are your prospective competitors doing? You can't always follow the crowd, but you need to know what the crowd is doing. Success is earned by the bold, who have a good business plan. Then step a little into the unknown or take a measured risk. As you implement your plan, make adjustments as necessary and push forward, the risks will probably be easier to address. There is almost always going to be some risk around most entrepreneurial activities. Sometimes the risk is near, sometimes it is far away. Some of us might trip and fall into the unknown risks of business. But if we get up and brush off our knees, we might find the severity of the risk has been reduced, because we have gained experience, which will help us deal with the unknowns. Each experience can help you be prepared for the next step in your progress. You will build experience along the path.

For those of you with an existing Farmers' Market business and you want to add a new product line or open a second Farmers' Market location, etc, the same advice applies.

## QUESTIONS:

**What do you see in the future that makes you fearful?**

_____

_____

_____

_____

**What opportunities do you see in the future?**

_____

_____

_____

_____

## How will you handle risk?

_____

_____

_____

_____

# TOPIC 6

## WHAT YOU WILL NEED TO GET STARTED

First and foremost, you will need a great product that meets the following criteria:

• An appealing appearance

• A great taste (if a food product)

• A competitive price

• Very high quality

• Something people need or want, and will purchase

• A product made by the vendor or purchased (depending on rules of your Farmers Market). Some markets require all goods to be made by the vendor. Check with your target market.

Well, I believe the criteria listed above are obvious, but it does not hurt to make sure.

Now the other things:

• A sturdy, clean canopy. These can be purchased online or at big box stores such as Walmart ™, Home Depot ™, Lowes ™, etc.

o You will also need hold-down anchors such as sand bags or cement blocks, etc. You don't want your canopy to fly off like a kite in a strong gust of wind. Make sure the anchors are not trip hazards.

• Several sturdy, but light weight tables to display your items.

• Several colorful tablecloths (or maybe new bedsheets) to cover your tables. This is a nice touch to set you apart from other vendors.

• A very good ice chest if you have food items.

• Possibly dry ice for food.

• A fold up chair.

• A credit card reader and merchant account for your cell phone or tablet so as to accept credit card payments.

• A small cash box.

• Signs (big and small) as appropriate.

• Maybe a Sterno ™ or similar heat source for keeping sample foods warm.

• Plastic or paper bags or small bakery boxes as appropriate, for your customers to carry away your goods.

• Tote Boxes to carry your goods to the market, etc. These can be tucked away under a draped table.

• Some cash for change.

• Business Cards and a holder for your table.

• A note pad for customers to leave their email addresses, etc.

• Samples

The above items can be purchased for about $500 - $700. There are very few retail businesses in which you can set up shop for such a small investment, and expect to make some money.

Most vendors report it takes 30 to 60 minutes to set up on site and about an equal amount of time, or less, to take down their booth.

# TOPIC 7

# BUSINESS PLANS

Business plans can be simple or very elaborate.

I am a firm believer in the value of business plans. It often surprises me how often people start a small business without putting pen to paper (or keystroke to screen/monitor) to plan what they want to accomplish with their business and how they are going to achieve it. Actually, I would guess that most small businesses do NOT have a written business plan.

There is an old saying I like that pertains to setting goals: "A goal not written is merely a wish." The same is true of business plans. You can have good thoughts and intellectual plans, but if those thoughts are not written down, then it is difficult to follow up and those great ideas could be lost and forgotten.

It is not my intent to tell you the procedures for writing a business plan that fits your needs. Those instructions are available on the internet and/or at your local book store or library. However, it is my intent to encourage you to develop a business plan that will enhance your opportunity for success. The complexity is up to you.

- Write your business plan. Simply thinking about it, is not enough. Put pen to paper!

• Give serious thought to its structure, content, follow up, timing, sales forecast and strategy for profitability, etc.

• There are tutorials and templates on the internet.

• Initially, review your business plan frequently – say monthly or more often. Once you get established, you will not need to review it as frequently. However, if you are adding a new product or service, and you have modified your business plan to accommodate the new product or service, it would be prudent to review the plan more often.

• Implement your business plan

• Remember, your business plan is not carved in stone. It should be a living, changeable document that reflects your current business circumstances, as well as your potential. Make modifications as needed.

Obviously, having a business plan will not guarantee your business success. However, having a business plan will go a long way to enabling your business to succeed.


## QUESTIONS:


**When are you going to write your business plan?**

_____

_____

_____

_____

**How often will you review it initially?**

_____

_____

_____

# TOPIC 8

# BUSINESS CARDS

Every business should have business cards. The primary purpose for business cards is so your customers and prospective customers can contact you. A secondary, but important function is a means to introduce you and your business.

I am often surprised by how the primary function was overlooked when designing and/or laying out the information that will be on the card. People use strange fonts that are difficult to read, or the font is too small. Often on color business cards, there is too little contrast between the printed words and the background making it difficult to distinguish the phone number (is that a 6 or an 8?) or determine the correct email address, etc. Think of your business card as a mini billboard. You have about 5 seconds or less to convey your message.

The following are the basics that should be achieved on your business card:

- The overall card has to be attractive (balanced) and easy to read.
- The font needs to be crisp.
- The font has to be large enough to be easily read. A combination of font sizes is attractive. For example, the company name or

your name could be a larger font and bolded.

- Basic data needs to be there:
  - Company name
  - What your business does. An extensive list is not necessary. However, if you think a list is necessary; print it on the back of the card.
    - o Your name
    - o Contact phone numbers:
      - Mobile
      - Office
      - Email address, plus maybe indicate you are on Facebook, Pinterest, Twitter, etc (tradenames).
      - Your website
  - Other things you might do to distinguish your card:
    - Use colors
    - Use borders on the edges of the card
    - Picture of product, such as a cupcake or pie if you are a baker and that is your specialty.
    - Address

Do not overcrowd the card. Remember it is not a book. It is to give basic information to your customers and prospective customers so they can contact you and know the nature of your business.

If your current business card does not measure up to expectations, discard it and start again. Show proofs to family and friends for their feedback prior to ordering several hundred new cards. When you are not there, your business card will represent you to the buyer. Make sure it properly reflects **YOU!**

The standard size for a rectangular business card is 2 X 5.5 inches. However, I'm starting to see square business cards measuring 2 7/8 X 2 7/8 inches. This new size is unique, but remember it will not easily "nest" with existing cards your customer may be saving. You will have to judge if this is a concern for you. Another consideration is to print your information vertically versus horizontally as on a conventional business card. Another thing you can do to make your cards unique is to have the corners cut into curves or angles.

You can purchase business cards at business supply stores. They will design a card for you at a reasonable fee. Usually, you can make one or two changes before they charge an extra fee – a matter of a few dollars. Several printing companies have online programs with free graphics and formats. If you want a unique or complicated design, you might have to contact a graphic designer to design your card.

Business cards are important, so spend the time and money that will get you an effective card. Before your cards are printed, you will receive an electronic proof for your approval. Carefully review the content and layout to ensure it meets your objectives.

Once you give your approval and 500 cards have been printed, if you find a mistake, it is your problem, not the printer's. It can be an expensive and embarrassing lesson – avoid it.

Freely hand out your business cards. You designed them and bought them to give away. Make sure your business cards are on your display table. Always carry some of your business cards with you on your daily activities. You never know when a business opportunity will present itself. You want to be ready to take advantage of the opportunity and hand out your business card and discuss your business.

I once heard a great definition of "luck". Luck is where opportunity and preparation meet. So if you have an opportunity, and you do not have your business card with you, then you did not experience luck. You were not prepared for luck. You might have missed an opportunity.

Consider putting a business card in every shopping bag a customer takes away.

## QUESTION

**What data are you going to include on your business card?**

_____

_____

_____

_____

_____

_____

_____

_____

# TOPIC 9

# BOOKKEEPING / ACCOUNTING

I hate to keep financial books. But for those of you who do not mind doing your own financial books, there are many over the counter computer programs that can make this necessary and important business function easier to accomplish. You can find such programs in a good office supply store or on the internet.

An important thing to do is to keep all of your business related receipts, bank statements, and other financial papers or documents. Do not throw away these records. Set up folders for each category you will need (banking, expenses, materials, equipment, etc) and put the specific paper work into these folders. This will make keeping your financial books easier to do.

The timely maintaining of your business records will allow you to format and print financial reports, which will tell you how you are doing financially. Are you making a profit? How much? Or it will give you the bad news that you are losing money. Reports can tell you where you are spending money and allow you to determine if you are spending too much or too little. A good report format will even tell you what is selling well. Good bookkeeping will make filing your federal, state and local income taxes easier (but probably not more enjoyable).

For those of you who don't like to keep books, there is a simple solution which I have used for years. I hire a part time bookkeeper as an independent contractor. I have one primary folder entitled "Bookkeeper", into which goes all the current paperwork (receipts, expense, bills, invoices, etc). If I think the bookkeeper needs specific information about a receipt, I just write a note on it explaining the situation and pass it on to the bookkeeper. In addition, I send a photocopy of my check register to the bookkeeper. In the actual register, I draw a heavy line to indicate at what point I photocopied the data. The next time I send data to the bookkeeper, I know where to start photocopying. Of course, one should put a short, but good explanation for the expenditure in the register. The bookkeeper has set up the necessary electronic files for my business on his/her computer. The bookkeeper enters the data from the referenced folder into the computer. As each piece of data is entered into the bookkeeper's computer, she/he puts a check mark on the appropriate paper indicating to me that the data has been entered. The bookkeeper then returns the paper data to me and I file it into specific folders (banking, expenses, utilities, etc., as indicated above). The data the bookkeeper entered into his/her computer is now available to me through the internet. I can then format and print financial reports as needed.

CPAs (Certified Public Accountants) handle significantly more difficult matters than simple entry of data. CPAs primarily audit companies' books for accuracy and fraud, annually close the books, and they also handle income tax preparation. CPAs can offer valuable advice on expanding your business if you have moved beyond a couple of Farmers Market booths.

Bookkeepers normally will charge you a reasonable fee for their services. In most cases, a bookkeeper will easily be able to do the books for a Farmers Market business.

Obviously, you never co-mingle your business revenue with your personal checking/savings accounts. You will need to set up a separate bank account for your business and run all your business transactions through that account.

## QUESTION:

**Are you going to do the financial books yourself or hire a bookkeeper to do the books for you?**

_____

_____

# TOPIC 10

# CREDIT AND DEBIT CARDS

In today's electronic age, there is no need to have electricity at your booth in order to conduct business. Yes, we will still need a secure physical box to hold cash. But an increasing number of customers will use credit or debit cards to make their purchases. However, to take advantage of this technology, you will need to have a smart phone or tablet etc, which has the capability to connect wirelessly to the Internet. The type of system (Android ™, etc.) does not matter.

There are a small number of manufacturers who produce credit/debit card readers that will manually attach (swipe type cards) or Blue Tooth connect (chip type cards) to your smart phone etc. The vendor simply swipes the buyers card through the reader or inserts the chip card into the reader and the transaction is recorded. The customer acknowledges the sale, by signing their name via their finger across the screen of your smart phone etc. The money from the sale is then transferred to your bank account. There is a small fee for this service.

For more information on credit card readers, google or use some other search engine for "Small Credit Card Readers for

Smartphones" to get a list of businesses who can provide you with these products/services. Then thoroughly explore all of your options before you enter into any agreement.

In today's business world, the acceptance of credit/debit cards is absolutely essential to maximize your sales.

The fraudulent use of credit cards has become a major financial problem for the credit card industry. Most of Europe and Asia have incorporated enhanced safety in the use of Credit Cards which has reduced the incidences of fraud, whereas the USA has lagged behind in this endeavor. However, that is now changing. A new standard of operation has been developed, which is called EMV (Europe, MasterCard, Visa) to be a more secure way of purchasing using credit/debit cards. Every customer's credit/debit card will have its own embedded microchip. The microchip is essentially a small computer, which makes it much more difficult to replicate the card, therefore significantly reducing the incidences of fraudulent use of credit/debit cards. Basically, the microchip creates a unique impression every time the card is used.

## QUESTION:

**What credit card reader are you going to use and why?**

---

---

---

---

# TOPIC 11

# MARKETING AND ADVERTISING

One of the distinct advantages of having a Farmers Market business is that you do not have to pay for advertising. But that does not mean you do not need to advertise!

We live in the electronic age and the internet and social media give us access to hundreds, maybe thousands or tens of thousands of potential buyers (customers), basically for free. Make sure everyone on your social media list, (and email list) who lives within driving distance of your Farmers Market booth, knows you have a Farmers Market business. Ask your contacts to also spread the word with their social media contacts (Facebook ™, LinkedIn ™, etc). Of course you should also have a link in your message that links to your specialized social media page dedicated to your business. That page should give detailed information where your Farmers Market booth is located, days and hours of operation as well as specific information about your product line and how to order product. You should send out details about your business on a regular basis, telling about new products, specials, closeouts, etc. You could even offer a small discount if they reference your website or social media page, when they make a purchase at your Farmers Market booth. In addition to the electronic media that needs to be used, there are also the physical needs of advertising, which include banners, displays and overall presentation. Additionally, you will need to solicit customers to stop at your booth by initiating a conversation as prospective customers walk by – such as would you like a sample etc. (See sections – Websites and Other Electronic Media, and – Presentation).

The strategy outlined above is really a simple example of the basic definition of a marketing plan, which is a process of promoting, selling and distributing a product or service.

Now for those of you who want to expand into retail outlets, the marketing plan becomes more involved and it might include advertising expenses (flyers, tastings at retail outlets, etc.). For example, if you have a food product, you will have to utilize a commercial kitchen (see section: Cottage Food Act and Commercial or Commissary Kitchens). Or if you have a non-food product, you will have to determine how you are going to produce the volume necessary to stock several retail outlets and finance that inventory.

If you are going to do any business with retail outlets, you will have to determine who your potential customers (types of businesses, etc.) are going to be, who you will contact, how you will get an appointment, and what you are going to tell them. For more details on this line of thinking, please see the following topics: Business Plans; Samples, Spiels and Sales; Desire and Passion; Incubators – For Serious Entrepreneurs; and No Usually Means Not Today.

**QUESTIONS:**

**How will you market your product – the simple way?**

_____

_____

_____

**How will you market your product – the more involved way?**

_____

_____

_____

# TOPIC 12

# WEBSITES AND OTHER ELECTRONIC MEDIA

We live in the electronic age, which means vast amounts of information are available to almost everyone. Additionally, we have become accustomed to instant communication through social media as well as texting, email and cell phone services. Our customers want information about the product they might buy, as well as the business that is selling the product. Customers want to make purchases from the comfort of their homes, maybe at unconventional times, such as holidays at 2:00 am.

A website can be informational and also serve as a 24/7, always open store and allows you to present the information requested about your products and business and capture the sale. Online purchasing (e-commerce) is growing each year. According to the US Census Bureau, "The first quarter 2015 e-commerce estimate increased 14.5% from the first quarter of 2014, while total retail sales increased 1.6% in the same period. E-commerce sales in the 1st quarter of 2015 accounted for 7.1% of total sales." Also bear in mind that a large percentage of customers, have at least looked at the product on the vendor's website before they made the actual purchase at the store or vendor booth. This is particularly true for large dollar value purchases. Having a website is an opportunity to provide more detailed information than you might be able to do in a face to face situation with the customer.

There are very few businesses in today's world that can be without a viable website. Note I said viable. The site has to be user friendly and effective.

When designing your website, which is meant to inform and sell, always evaluate the operation and layout from the perspective of the potential customer. Ask yourself "What is the customer looking for and hoping to find?" and "Where will the customer expect to find the information?"

Then determine how you are going to design the website to help the customer and also meet your own objectives for the site. Put these mutual objectives in writing and discuss the list with your web designer. Review competitors' sites and ask yourself what you can do better. Also determine what good aspects of their sites you can incorporate into your site.

There are many internet sites which can help you to design and develop you own website. Or you can contract with a local website designer and meet face to face to discuss your objectives in detail. If you do meet with a web designer, make sure to review sites he/she has designed and ask for references.

Some capabilities to include in your site would be SEO (Search Engine Optimization), which use key words to help improve how quickly and consistently people searching the internet find your website. Discuss this in detail with your web designer. You should also have a search function, list links to blogs, photos and descriptions of your products and of course a shopping cart function that will allow the customer to make a purchase.

It would also be productive to have an area for customer comments. If the comments are good, it could lead to additional business. On the other hand if the comments are negative, you could lose business. Therefore, keep your customers happy. Make sure your website is "mobile phone" friendly.

Before you actually launch the site, ask friends and others who might be knowledgeable to review the site for glitches, grammar, content, spelling errors, ease of use, etc. You want them to be brutally honest with their comments. This will help you and your designer to develop a more effective website.

A viable website should represent you and become your most important electronic media sales tool. It will be a tireless worker representing you 24 hours a day, seven days a week. It will not take off work for any holidays or go on vacation. But if you do not maintain it correctly, either by yourself or by a professional, the site might take unexpected and potentially catastrophic sick leave, by crashing. Avoid this.

To direct potential customers to your website, you will need to be an active participant in social media such as Facebook ™, LinkedIn ™, etc. Make sure your contacts know about your business and have links to your website. Ask them to "like" your site. Ask your contacts to tell their contacts about your business and provide a link to your website.

You might also consider writing a "blog" about the nature of your business. For example, if you sell baked goods, then a blog about cooking might be interesting to your contacts, especially if you include recipes, reviews, or explain specific techniques such as how to make great, flaky pie crust for example. You can write in general terms or be specific.

These three electronic legs (website, social media, and blogs) can be the business platform to improve your profitability and success.

## QUESTIONS:

**Will you design your own website (through an online program) or hire a professional website designer?**

_____

**How are you going to find a web designer?**

_____

_____

_____

**What are your website objectives?**

_____

_____

_____

_____

_____

**How will you use social media to your business advantage?**

_____

_____

_____

_____

_____

# SECTION 3

# Farmers Markets.

# The Details

# TOPIC 13

# PART-TIME OR FULL-TIME

One of the attractive things about owning and operating a Farmers Market business is, for the most part, that it is a part-time work environment during the warm part of the year. Most Farmers Markets will be held on a Saturday morning or early afternoon. This arrangement allows the Farmers Market operator to hold a full-time job during weekdays. It also allows necessary preparation time for the weekend Farmers Market.

However, depending on where you live, there might be several Farmers Market locations that meet during the week. I live near Denver Colorado and there are Farmers Markets within 60 miles that meet somewhere, every single day of the week during the spring, summer and fall.

Therefore, if just having a booth on one day is not enough action for you, then you might be able to conduct business at several different locations throughout the week. Most states publish an annual guide to Farmers Markets located in that state. The guide will tell you meeting places, times and days of the week, and also list phone numbers and/or websites pertinent to that specific location. Of course you can also search for Farmers Market sites near you, on the internet.

This option of Farmers Markets meeting during the week is particularly important if running a Farmers Market booth is going to be your primary source of income. I know of an older man (about 65 years old) who sells kettle corn and home-made root beer. He has been doing this for many years. He has Farmers Market booths five days a week. Bear in mind that most Farmers Markets are only open 4 to 5 hours per day. In some cases, he drives over 100 miles to participate in a Farmers Market.

An advantage of working multiple days is that if you have to take a day off, you can have a family member or friend run your booth for you or just not open on that specific day. Another option for consideration, if there are several Farmers Markets in your area and they all meet on the same day, is to utilize a business partner, or enlist the assistance of a spouse, or sibling, or older children to operate the booth at a neighboring location. This arrangement could be very financially rewarding. See section on "Family Involvement."

Of course, if you have a product that you are trying to get into conventional retail outlets, it goes without saying you are going to be working longer hours. Take Richard for example. He opened a Farmers Market booth to sell a family recipe of a regional salad dressing. His Farmers Market booth was so successful that he quit his regular job and started working full time at developing and improving his primary product. He then started developing additional products and flavors. He now uses a commercial kitchen (see section on commercial kitchens) to produce his products and sells them in several states via a national retailer.

## QUESTION:

**Where and when do Farmers Markets meet near you – say within 100 miles (or further if you choose)?**

_____

_____

_____

_____

# TOPIC 14

## SAMPLES, SPIELS AND SALES

**Samples:**

I have had many Farmers Market Vendors tell me that having samples is the key to their success. This is particularly true for food vendors who want to make sales, but it is also applicable for other vendors, who sell such items as soaps and lotions.

Sample sizes should be big enough to spark an interest for more, but not large enough to extinguish the spark. For food samples, check with your local health department regarding any restrictions pertaining to the dissemination of samples.

A sample allows the prospective customer to satisfy their initial curiosity. And if a prospective customer is curious enough to stop at your booth, then it gives you, the Farmers Market Vendor, the opportunity to impress and "wow" the prospect, while at the same time verbalizing the attributes of the product to reinforce the good taste, feel, or other sensations the prospect is experiencing, and thereby make the sale.

I saw an interesting and effective sample presentation. The vendor sold pies of various flavors/ingredients. For her sample presentation, she coarsely mashed up a pie, and then dipped a small sample spoon into the results. This would give the prospective customer a taste of the crust and the ingredients. She then arranged the spoons full of samples on a large platter in a circular pattern, along with the samples of several other pie flavors. This provided a very nice visual presentation and an effective way for the prospective customers to get representative tastes of several different pie flavors. .

I also saw a vendor with a unique way of keeping his food samples cool. He had put ice packs into a metal pan (about 10" X 10") with 2 inch high sides. This was covered with a colorful cloth. On top of this was a 12" X 12" marble tile. In the center area of the tile he had arranged his candy samples. The marble tile was kept cool by the ice, which in turn, kept the samples cool, plus it gave an attractive display.

**Spiels:**

Successful salespeople have several well thought out and practiced spiels about their products or services. The spiel needs to be short, but powerful, with the objective to help the customer  decide to purchase your product, and feel good about the purchase. Spiels can be about how the product was developed or where it comes from etc., such as (1) "This is my grandmother's recipe and all of our family loves it!  Isn't it good?" or something such as (2) "We only use chocolate with 80% or more cacao content. That is what gives it such a deep, rich, full-bodied flavor."

Now, let's do a little analysis of these two spiels:

• The first spiel:

oThe use of the word "grandmother" most likely will bring memories, hopefully good memories, of the prospect's grandmother, to the mind of the prospect, thereby being a positive reinforcement of the experience.

o The use of the word "family" almost always reinforces the positive experience. Family is a powerful word and might get the prospect to agree with you.

o "Isn't it good?" Well your product better be good, or you will never succeed. (I just remembered as a boy using a popular brand of mouthwash. It had a terrible taste, but sold by the millions. But the company had millions of dollars to spend on promotion and advertising the other attributes to overcome the bad taste. But we do not have millions of dollars, so Farmers Markets products had better be good and of high quality.) What you want to do is ask questions that will get the prospect to agree with you – to say YES! If you can get a customer to say yes to a few questions, there is a higher probability they will say yes, when you ask them to buy.

• The second spiel:

o The 80% cacao statement infers quality. The prospect agrees with the follow up comment about "rich, full-bodied flavor". This reinforces the taste still in the prospects mouth. Now is the time to ask the "sale" question.

• Some thought starter spiels applicable to various types of vendors might include:

  • You're just in time:

    o Everything is for sale!

    o Everything is fresh!

    o Everything you see (is/was):

- Painted/Drawn (etc) by a great artist!
- Baked by a great cook!
- Tastes great!
- Made by hand.
- Designed by me!
- Made locally.
- Etc.

## Sales:

The other thing successful sales people do is ask for the sale. Certainly, many customers will make an impulse purchase, and we welcome those sales. But a great many prospects are "willing" to make a purchase (they have stopped to look, taste, feel, etc.) but they need a little psychological nudge to buy. If you learn to ask for the sale, you might very well go from having a "good" sales day, to having a "great" sales day.

You might consider offering a bulk deal, such as "4 for $20" or BOGO (buy one get one free), etc.

Never be embarrassed to ask for the sale, such as asking, "How many would you like?", or "Wouldn't that be good for dinner tonight?" etc.

Obviously, there are some people who have been born with a "honey" tongue, with a natural gift to become a salesperson. But most salespeople are not so naturally gifted. Sales is a profession. And like any profession, successful sales techniques can be learned. Yet, like any profession, one does need some inclination for that specific profession.

If you have a desire to own and operate your own business and to interact with people, you are probably inclined to be a salesperson. This is particularly effective when you harness that inclination with ambition, desire and training. You can learn to become a salesperson. There are plenty of books and on-line videos that can teach you the skills of successful salespeople.

Remember, you are in business to make sales – not just one, but many sales. Making sales are why you made the product, spent time developing your business, risked your capital, etc.

Bear in mind, you have a wonderful product that is going to benefit your customer. You are helping them spend their money wisely, to improve their quality of life, save them time, etc, etc. Ask for the sale!

It is very important to greet every prospective customer with a smile and a quick spiel, such as:    "We have great cookies (or whatever) today.", or "Our cookies (or whatever) are made with real butter."

## QUESTIONS:

**What are your spiels going to be?**

_____

_____

_____

_____

**How will you ask for the sale?**

_____

_____

_____

_____

**How many times per day are you going to practice your spiels until they become second nature?**

_____

**What sales training are you going to seek out and study?**

_____

_____

_____

# Topic 15

# PRESENTATION

Most of us have been told since our youth, "first impressions are lasting impressions." Well, this is certainly true in the business environment. We often form opinions of others by their form of dress, their neatness, how they speak, etc. These impressions are also important and influential in the Farmers Market environment.

The title of this section is presentation, so your thoughts might automatically go to the layout of your product on the display table. But there is more to it than that. Presentation is the whole environment of your booth.

Dress modestly and make sure you always wear a smile on your face. Use good manners and be courteous (see section "Manners and Courtesies".)

A good physical presentation will make it easier for your customers to find you and do business with you.

I suggest you have a banner ad attached to the rear (or front) of your canopy. This should be large enough and with a dark, crisp font, so as to be able to be clearly read from a distance.

Your products need to be clearly identified with a nice clean label in front of the specific products. Give your customers information to help them buy. For example if you are selling a handmade wooden product – give it a name and then identify what type of wood was used. If it is a sauce – identify if it is mild or spicy, for example.

Your product, particularly if it is a food product, might need individual labels listing ingredients, expiration date, etc. Research your specific state, county, city requirements. The acquisition of your food license might require that you identify these data.

Cover your display table with a colorful cloth (or combination of colors) such as crisscrossing different color flannel panels. But use what will best serve your display purposes.

Ah, now comes the hard part, the actual display of your products. I can't tell you how to best accomplish this. You are going to have to experiment. But there are some things you need to keep in mind.

• The display needs to be neat and orderly.

• The products have to be accessible to your customers.

• The display needs to be colorful to attract and guide the customer's eye. The texture of display media can also help accomplish this, such as woven baskets or wood.

• The products can be on shelves, colorful platforms or boxes, or spread out.

• Do not have unnecessary items on your display tables, such as a cash box, items under construction, your phone, etc. Only products that will help your customer buy should be on your display tables.

Be willing to experiment on your display layout. Ask other vendors or friends for their "honest" opinions. This is no time for them to be nice because they do not want to offend you. If the display is only mediocre, you need to know it so you can improve the display. You want a real opinion – the good, the bad and the ugly. But bear in mind, someone else's opinion might not be correct. You need to judge each opinion on its merits and not just make a change without your own assessment that the change will improve the display. Others' opinions should help you evaluate the situation and look at it from a different point of view.

Learn from others – how do your competitors and other vendors display their products? Ask yourself what you can learn from their displays and incorporate, or avoid in your display presentation.

I had a vendor tell me she often changes her display in an effort to improve it. Sometimes, she prominently displays a product she really wants to sell, etc. She takes photos of each set-up and keeps a copy in a folder she always has with her. She refers to these photos when she sets up her booth.

## QUESTION:

**How will you judge and improve your display presentation?**

_____

_____

# Topic 16

# MANNERS AND COURTESIES

It amazes me how business people (and if you have a booth at a Farmers Market – you are a business person) need to be reminded to use good manners, particularly when dealing with potential customers.

Yet, some still seem oblivious to saying: "please, thank you, can I help you, etc." Be courteous. If you are sitting, stand when a potential customer is before you. Smile! A customer is not an inconvenience to you. That customer is the whole reason you are in business. If the customer does not feel welcome or appreciated; he/she does not care how great your product or price is. He/She will take their business where it is appreciated. Most of us cannot afford to lose any customers. We need to take the opportunity to teach a potential customer about our product or service. An informed customer is a better customer. A nice touch that also provides positive reinforcement for future business is to say, "Thank you. See you next week."

Be friendly and courteous. Have a smile on your face and acknowledge your potential customer. This will go a long way to help you become successful.

People like to look each other in the eye when they are talking, particularly when conducting business. If the eyes of the seller are hidden behind dark sunglasses, the buyer might be uneasy. We cannot afford that negative feeling because the customer might not come back. So if it is a sunny day and you are wearing sunglasses, I recommend that you take them off when you approach your potential customer.

You want to conduct yourself so as to avoid potential offense to a customer. It is easier to avoid an offense, than it is to correct or overcome, even an unintentional offense. It is best to assume your customer lives by very high standards. Therefore, when trying to conduct business, do not smoke, chew gum or wear offensive or immodest clothing. It is a small inconvenience to avoid doing these things, so as to improve your probability of making a sale and more importantly, making a happy customer who might make repeat purchases.

## QUESTION:

**What are you going to do to avoid offending a potential customer?**

_____

_____

_____

# Topic 17

# CUSTOMERS AND COMPETITIVE POSITION

**Customers:**

In any successful business, it helps in the planning mode, to identify your prospective customers. There are a myriad of questions, such as:

- Where will the customers come from?
- How will the customers find your business?
- What are their quality and pricing expectations?
- How frequently will they shop?
- How much will they spend?
- What is their economic position?
- Will they use cash or credit/debit cards?
- Etc.

The above questions are pertinent to most businesses. But for the Farmers Market vendor they are generally answered in a positive manner, just because of the Farmers Market environment. However, some questions may be very specific to your product. You will have to determine those particular questions and access the answers and adjust as necessary.

Basically, attendees to Farmers Markets come from most spectrums of life. Most will come with the intent to buy, but some will come just to enjoy the vibrant environment of the Farmers Market. You must be prepared to attract your prospective customers (see Samples, Spiels and Sales) to your booth  With experience and time, you will build up a clientele of repeat customers. Believe me, repeat customers are the life blood of most companies.

Competitive Position:

Probably, the first thing one thinks of when talking about competitive position is relative to the price of the product. But competitive position is much more, such as:

• The quality of your product.

• The quality of the service you provide. (See Manners and Courtesies).

• Your presentation

• Your welcoming attitude

• Etc.

Let's look at price. I personally see no need to be the lowest priced provider. I prefer to be priced in the midrange. But if you have superior quality, or uniqueness, or excellent service and ambience, then customers are usually willing to pay more for the product.

Good quality service is almost as important as the quality of the product. Customers want to be appreciated and also want to feel they are making the right decision to buy from you, versus the other vendor down the street.

A good booth presentation will go a long way to encourage a prospective customer to investigate your products and discuss the product's attributes with you.

A successful competitive position is when, through your marketing plan, you have combined all the above variables so the customer is willing and happy to purchase your product.

## QUESTIONS:

### Who are your Customers?

_____

_____

_____

_____

### What will you do to be competitive?

_____

_____

_____

# Topic 18

# SELECTING YOUR PRODUCTS TO SELL

### Food Items - Recipes

Obviously, the Internet is a prime source of finding recipes. Plus there are a plethora of cookbooks available at libraries or the local bookstore. In some cases you will have to adjust the recipes for large batches. This is best achieved by baking or cooking a large batch and then doing a taste test with your family and/or friends. Make sure you get honest opinions, so you can further refine the recipe.

However, the best place to find the right food item for marketing at the Farmers Market is in your own kitchen or the kitchen of your Mother or Grandmother or Mother-in-Law, or friend. Do not give this just a cursory thought, but really think about those sumptuous items you have enjoyed eating, within your sphere. I bet there is someone you know who makes some really delicious food products. Ask them to share the recipe with you or better yet, ask them to help you cook a batch. Who knows, maybe this person will be a willing collaborator in your Farmers Market venture. But find a food product that you love the flavor of, that is savory and hopefully unique.

However, remember, a lot of people make great brownies or chocolate chip cookies and sell lots of them profitably. But most of these "common" products are unique because the cook has, as my Mother used to say, "doctored them up". They have used butter instead of margarine, cream or half and half instead of milk, fresh tomatoes instead of canned, fresh ground spices instead of bottled, etc. Or they have added some unique things, such as macadamia nuts or mint chocolate.

I remember going to a church social event where refreshments were served. I can still remember the sumptuous brownies the preacher's wife served. They were indeed "doctored up". They were covered with a wonderful creamy chocolate icing, which was decorated with an interesting design. The brownie was thick and moist, with a deep dark color and was very flavorful. There were pieces of walnuts in the batter. Her plate of brownies was always the first to be emptied on the serving table. As I remember those savory brownies, I wish I had her recipe so I could bake a batch.

Other Products:

The lists of various products in the topic "What's For Sale At Farmers Markets" can get you started on finding a product to market. Evaluate the lists carefully. Also consider what you might like to buy at a Farmers Market but have not been able to find for sale there. If you want it, others might want it as well.

Whatever product you decide to sell at your Farmers Market, it is very important you have a significant interest in that product. If you are not excited about it or if you don't believe it can solve your customers' problems or meet their desires and expectations, you are probably not going to succeed. Once you have identified that product, then you have to diligently search the internet for suppliers or fabricate it yourself. If you are going to sell a prefabricated product then you will have to contact the supplier to determine availability, costs (payment terms), quality, durability, and delivery etc.

## QUESTIONS:

**What are your favorite recipes you could use in a Farmers Market?**

_____

_____

_____

_____

**What great foods are your mother, mother-in-law, grandmother, etc. known for?**

_____

_____

_____

_____

_____

**What friends make great foods?  What are the foods?**

_____

_____

_____

_____


**What food products are you going to consider selling at the Farmers Market?**

_____

_____


**What products would you like to buy at a Farmers Market, but cannot find?**

_____

_____

_____

# Topic 19

# DEALING WITH RETURNS

Nobody wants an unhappy customer. Most Farmers Market vendors I have interviewed have not had very many returns of goods. Lack of "returns" is primarily because the vendor sells a high quality product. But simply the lack of returns is not a 100% assurance of high quality of product or services. Sometimes the customer considers it too much trouble to return the product. This customer will simply not do any more business with you.

As a business owner, it is important to have a policy regarding how you are going to handle returns. Most vendors will offer an exchange for a replacement item of equal or greater value; most vendors want to avoid refunding cash. But if that is the only alternative to keep a happy customer, then that is what you will have to do.

When someone returns an item, there are two objectives you must have:

1.     Keep that customer happy so they will continue to buy from you. This is best handled by happily meeting the customer's

expectation of service and solving their problem, either through
exchange or refund. It is also very important to apologize for their
inconvenience.

2.     Why is the product being returned? The answer to this
question needs to be arrived at tactfully. Normally, if a customer is
returning a product, there is something wrong with it. You need to
find out what the problem is. This is very valuable information,
because the correction of that problem could help you to have a
better product. When the customer is gone, determine what changes
to your process you can implement to correct the problem. However,
bear in mind your changes to your process, must be improvements
and not introduce more problems. (See section on Continuous
Improvement),

## QUESTION:

**How will you deal with returns?**

_____

_____

_____

# Topic 20

# MATS AND/OR CARPETS

Since most Farmers Markets are held on a hard, paved surface (streets, parking lots, etc.), it is to your advantage if you can make your booth more comfortable for your clientele. This should increase their probability of making a purchase. For example, you can lay a carpet on the ground under your canopy.

I remember one time walking down a long row of booths. My feet were noticeably tired. As I stepped in front of a booth, my feet were greeted with softness. The vendor had used large (2' X 2' X ¼") interlocking rubber mats that extended about 2 feet in front of his booth. It was comfortable to stand there in front of his booth and conduct business. To reduce a trip hazard, the perimeter of the mats (again about ¼" thick) used tapered interlocking edge pieces. The vendor also extended the mats into the work space, so he too enjoyed the softness beneath his feet.

This brings up a good point. If you are going to be standing for four to six hours on asphalt or cement, a padded surface will go a long way to keep you fresh and energetic.

Whatever type of padding you are going to use, MAKE SURE
you reduce trip hazards by using proper trim pieces and/or tape
down the carpets, etc.

An advantage of using the interlocking rubber mats is that they are
easy to store and transport, as well as easy to assemble and
disassemble. They can also be closely sized to your particular canopy
and layout.

## QUESTION:

**What kind of floor covering are you going to use to increase
your and your customer's comfort level?**

_____

_____

_____

# Topic 21

# MUSIC AT FARMERS MARKETS

One of the enjoyable things about attending local Farmers Markets is that you might find instrumentalists or singers, performing along the street of vendors. This is particularly true at larger Farmers Markets.

At several of the large Farmers Markets I have attended, several spots are designated for such performances. The performers pre-register with the Farmers Market management and are assigned a designated spot and time. For example, spot #37, from 9:00 to 10:00. Some other performer will be assigned from 10:00 to 11:00, etc. onward to the close of the market. The performers are allowed to set out a donation/tip receptacle and hand out business cards and flyers.

Depending on the quality of the performance and the number of attendees, performers can pick-up $50, $100, $150+ in donations/tips. But more importantly, they can sell their CDs, tell where they are currently performing and what specialty work they can do, such as parties or weddings. They get to talk to their listeners and interact with shoppers in a more relaxed atmosphere than in a noisy, dark club venue.

Farmers Markets are profitable venues often overlooked by audio performers.

Music performers at the Farmers Market can be an advantage or disadvantage for the vendors whose booths are adjacent to these entertainers. If large groups of people gather around the entertainers, they might block access to your booth for your potential customers. If this is the case, talk to the market manager for assistance. On the other hand, the entertainers might draw people to them who will stop at your booth and maybe buy from you.

## QUESTION:

**Who do you know who might profit from performing at a Farmers Market?**

_____

_____

_____

# Topic 22

# FAMILY INVOLVEMENT

Owning and operating a Farmers Market business is an excellent opportunity to involve your family in the business. The involvement can be minimal to extensive. It is up to you, and of course the family member or members.

One booth operator I interviewed, who sells unique handmade soaps, asks her teenage children to help her name her soaps. Another booth operator has his family to thank for the idea of his business. He is a retired dentist, so his children are adults. One night at a family dinner, he served his uniquely formulated pepper/chili spread, which has a nice fire, but also is wonderfully flavorful. His son said it was so good that it should be marketed, hence, his involvement in a Farmers Market business. He has now expanded his business. In addition to his Farmers Market booth, he is also selling his pepper/chili spread to various retail grocery outlets. His family holds monthly business meetings, where his adult children have various responsibilities in managing the business.

If you have young or teenage children, getting them involved in your Farmers Market business could be a great training opportunity for them. They can have a "hands on" learning experience, which teaches them the basics of operating a business. You might be training a future entrepreneur!

The only suggestion I have is, that you should not force the issue of "involvement" on your family. Remember, this is your business, your dream.

Basically, the extent of involvement of your family in your business is up to you.

## QUESTIONS:

**How are you going to involve your family in your business?**

_____

_____

_____

**Who is most likely to want to participate?**

_____

_____

_____

**What jobs can they do?**

_____

_____

**If family is not available or willing to help, is there a friend who might want to participate in the business?  Who?**

_____

_____

# Topic 23

# WHAT VENDORS ARE DOING TO IMPROVE THEIR BUSINESSES

From my experience in the world of business, I am convinced that almost any process or design can be improved. Business is really just a series of processes. Now, a word of warning. Just because a process or design can be improved, does not mean it should be. There might be mitigating circumstances that negate the improvements – increased cost, delay in delivery, etc. Now don't let this warning throw you off the course of continuous improvement. Be selective in your improvements, but move ahead.

My bank has a Question of the Day, which is posted near the tellers (such as, "When was the first movie theater opened in the US and what was the cost of admission?". The customer makes a guess when at the teller. There is no reward, just the fun of getting the right answer or learning some bit of information. In this case, the answer was 1896 and $0.10 admission.

This concept could be used at your Farmers Market as a means to get passersby to stop at your booth. For example, if you were selling pet products, you might post a sign, with a question such as, "How many breeds are recognized by the American Kennel Club?." Or if you sold baked goods, you might ask, "How much flour is used in the USA every day?" etc. Each week you could have a different question. The objective is to get people to stop at your booth so you can talk to them.

Here are some things Farmers' Market vendors are doing to improve their business:

Julia, who sells custom sodas, pies and cookies says, "We evaluate our prices and products after each event. If there is anything that we've observed that hasn't sold for multiple events, we will remove it from our menu so as not to waste any costs by keeping extra inventory on hand."

Lisa, who sells pet foods and products and also has a store front, "works with the community to provide low cost shot clinics and toenail clips for pets. It is a fun event."

Johnelle, who makes and sells soaps, lotions, bath products and essential oils, "Visits other peoples' shops and booths, checks things on the internet, does soap challenges, watches videos, makes flyers, joined the Chamber of Commerce, has networking groups she attends, and posts photos of her creations on line."

Paul and Diane sell a specialized pepper spread. "They sent samples to all their friends and family to sample and help spread the word about their product. They participated in several city food and gift shows. They do food samplings at retail stores that sell their products. They visit store owners and ask them to sample their spread. If they like it, they ask the store owner to stock their product.

Richard, sells a regional salad dressing at Farmers Markets and also wholesales to regional super markets. He says "his brain is always 'on' about his business. He focuses on one product at a time and he focuses on building relationships with his customers."

Gypsy, who sells handcrafted jewelry and accessories, says "she will negotiate prices, make alternative recommendations, offer special orders to fit needs, and reuse customers old unused pieces and make them new. She offers discounts to repeat customers.

Dennis sells gourmet dip mixes, made of a wide variety of natural ingredients. When he first started, dip mixes were primarily used for chip dips. As people became more health conscience, he started marketing veggie dip mixes. His customers told him they also used his mixes in various recipes, such as gravies, stews, soups, etc. Now he passes this information to his prospective customers. It has become part of his spiel. He listened to his customers and applied what he had learned. He also has "tear and go" recipe cards on his booth display table – of course using his various dip mixes.

Kim offers loyalty cards to her customers. If the customer makes nine purchases of a specific product, the tenth one is free. By having a "loyalty card" in their wallet, the customer is continually reminded about that product and is induced to make an additional purchase, particularly as they get the seventh and eighth punch in their card.

One specialized soap vendor mounts small pieces of soap to popsicle sticks to allow customers to sniff the aroma of her soaps. She prints the name of the soap on the stick.

A lot of vendors are very active on social media asking friends to share the news and reviews of their products with their friends. They have great websites to inform and take orders.

Other Farmer Market vendors establish newsletters or blogs about their products and encourage their customers to "sign up" or subscribe at their booth to receive this data. This provides very beneficial information for the vendor and allows unique marketing to their existing customers.

## QUESTION:

**What are you going to do to improve your business?**

_____

_____

_____

_____

_____

_____

_____

# Topic 24

# FOOD STAMPS OR WELFARE ASSISTANCE

Yes, some (maybe most) Farmers Markets do accept Food Stamps or Welfare Assistance such as EBT, SNAP or whatever it is called in your area. This can be a good source of revenue. Most recipients of welfare assistance are given a unique "debit card" which allows electronic purchases by the recipient. Most Farmers Market vendors will normally accept credit/debit cards (see section on Credit Cards) in the course of doing business. However, welfare assistance cards have restrictions that limit utilization of the cards at certain Farmers Market vendor booths.

But Farmers Market Organizations have a way of making withdrawals against those welfare accounts. It works as follows:

• The welfare recipient goes to the booth organized by the Farmers Market managers/directors/supervisors and presents his/her welfare card.

• The management scans the card and withdraws money, specified by the recipient, in one dollar increments from the recipients account.

• The recipient then receives a wooden or metal token or some other manner of scrip, equal to the amount withdrawn from the account.

o The Farmers Market managers keep the cash until the vendors present the scrip for redemption.

• The recipient can then spend this "scrip" just like regular money with the vendors at the Farmers Market. However, there are usually restrictions (as shown below), but there might be others. So check with your local and state governments for restrictions specific to your area.

o Items that can be purchased with the scrip:

☐     Purchase of fresh fruits and vegetables.

☐     Purchase of dairy products

☐     Purchase of meat products

☐     Purchase of seeds

☐     Purchase of baked goods to be taken home.

☐     Purchase of plants intended for growing food.

o Items that can NOT be purchased with the scrip:

☐     Non-food items.

☐     Ready to eat foods.

☐     Hot foods

• Regular coin change can be given to the recipient, but vendors are encouraged to make up the difference "in product" to bring the purchase to whole dollar values of the scrip.

• At the end of the day, the vendor then takes the scrip received to the Farmers Market manager's booth and exchanges the scrip for normal currency.

# Topic 25

# BRICK AND MORTAR STORE FRONTS

At most Farmers Markets, you will often find one or more local, established retail businesses that have store fronts, warehouses, or other "brick and mortar" retail establishments, marketing their products/services through the Farmers Market.

There are many established (or struggling) store front businesses (bakeries, bike shops, pet food stores, etc.) that utilize Farmers Markets for several reasons. Here are a few:

• Expand their sales. They might reach a different customer base, which will need and use their product or service.

• Teach potential customers about their products or services. Farmers markets are great places to have a more relaxed opportunity to teach potential customers, in more detail, about your products and services.

• Direct potential customers to their retail establishments. A Farmers Market booth directs prospective customers to your store front. Although there might not be a specific sale at the Farmers

Market booth, the ultimate sale at the store front was generated at the Farmers Market. A Farmers Market booth lets the public know your business exists and brings people to the store front.

• Reduce competition. I had a Farmers Market vendor tell me they did not want their competitor, from a nearby town, to take their potential customers. It really would be a shame to allow a competitor to take your potential customers, (basically right from under your nose) when it could have been prevented if only the local retailer had taken better care of his/her market. This is especially true, with negative financial results, if one considers all the money a person invests in a retail store, which can be very expensive.

• Advertising. I had a vendor tell me that having a booth at a Farmers Market, at a cost of less than $50 a week was well worth the expense compared to the expense of other types of advertising. She was selling dog food, which is a recurring sale. She was getting between two and three new customers every week at the Farmers Market. Her other advertising was hardly generating any new customers compared to the expense. Lisa felt she "got more bang for her buck" for her advertising dollar by having a Farmers Market booth. Plus she got to meet and talk with prospective customers and educate them about the attributes of her dog food versus other retail conventional dog foods.

## QUESTION:

Do you or one of your associates have a store front that could benefit by also marketing through a Farmers Market booth?

_____

_____

_____

# Topic 26

# WINTER FARMERS MARKETS

I have fond memories of when I was a boy visiting the local Winter Farmers Market with my family. It was held in an abandoned railway station. In my mind, I can still smell the rich aroma of burning wood emitting from the two large pot-bellied stoves in the large room. Arrayed against the walls were vendors selling crafts as well as vendors with fresh baked goods and other items.

Winter Farmers Markets are becoming popular. They are held in a wide variety of venues, such as school auditoriums, cafeterias, and hallways, fairground exhibit halls, community buildings, and yes, even in railway stations. The important thing is, the venue is out of the cold weather, making it a comfortable and interesting area for prospective customers to shop and enjoy the atmosphere of the Farmers Market, even if it is snowing outside and the wind is howling. You can well imagine how much more inviting this venue is to the vendor! Usually there are fewer vendors, but that can mean less competition for your goods.

Winter weather does not eliminate your customers' needs and

desires for your products. Of course, the Winter Farmers Market gives the Farmers Market vendor an opportunity to sell his/her goods all through the year, thereby enhancing his/her income.

Even if you do participate in a winter market, it is still important you have a website so your customers can contact you and maybe buy from you.

## QUESTION:

**Is there a winter Farmers Market near you?  Where is it and are you going to participate?**

_____

_____

# SECTION 4

# Small Scale

# Entrepreneurship

# Topic 27

# COTTAGE FOOD ACT AND COMMERCIAL/COMMISSARY KITCHENS

Let's say you have found that perfect recipe for a food item you are confident the public will love and buy. Congratulations!

When you are first starting out, depending on the food item, you might be able to cook/prepare the item in your home kitchen. In most states, that law allowing home based cooking of food items is referred to as Cottage Food Act/Law. According to "<u>Cottage Food Laws in the United States</u>" by Harvard Food Law & Policy Clinic, (check the internet), only nine states (as of 2013) do not have formalized cottage food laws. But according to forager.com/law/, some of those states or districts within those states do allow producers to sell their homemade, low risk items to the public.

You will have to check the specific requirements in your area. Your target Farmers Market management should be able to provide specific guidance regarding the pertinent Cottage Food Act relative to that Farmers Market.

For all other food items not allowed by the pertinent Cottage Food Act, you will have to utilize the services of a state licensed Commercial or Commissary Kitchen. If your home based food item is successful and you cannot keep up the volume requirements in your home kitchen, the licensed Commercial or sometimes referred to as Commissary Kitchen is available to you

Let's talk about:

- **Cottage Food Act**. The data listed below is based on Colorado law, but it is representative of other states and is provided to give you an idea of the requirements. However, you will have to check the specifics of your state. The below is taken from the Colorado Department of Public Health and Environment, Division of Environmental Health and Sustainability, Retail Food Program.

  o Cottage food products include such non-potentially hazardous items as: spices, teas, dehydrated produce, nuts, seeds, honey, candies, jams, jellies and certain baked goods.

    ▪ Note: Non-potentially hazardous means: Any food or beverage that, when stored under normal conditions without refrigeration, will not support the rapid and progressive growth or microorganisms that cause food infections or food intoxications. Does not include low-acid or acidified foods, which must be produced in a licensed commercial kitchen.

o No license for the home kitchen is issued, nor is the home kitchen inspected. But it is subject to inspection by the state Department of Public Health and Environment if there are complaints about your product.

o Net sales for <u>each</u> product produced by cottage food operation must not exceed $5000 annually.

o Product must be sold directly by the cottage food operator to the end consumer.

o Sales by consignment or to retail food or wholesales food establishments are prohibited.

o Cottage food products must be labeled as follows:

  ▪ The producers name and address where the food item was prepared.

  ▪ The producers current phone number and email address.

  ▪ The date on which the food was produced

  ▪ A complete list of ingredients.

- And the following statement: "This product was produced in a home kitchen that is not subject to state licensure or inspection and that may also produce common food allergens such as tree nuts, peanuts, eggs, soy, wheat, milk, fish and crustacean shellfish. This product is not intended for resale."

o Cottage food producers are required "to take a food safety course that includes basic food handling training and is comparable to, or is a course given by, the Colorado State University Extension Service or a state, county, or district public health agency and must maintain a status of good standing in accordance with the course requirements, including attending any additional classes if necessary. Safe food handling courses should include topics on safe food sources, personal hygiene, sanitation of equipment, worker illness, food temperature control, safe water, sewage disposal, pest control, proper hand washing and control of toxins."

o Note: In addition to the above, there might also be additional requirements in your city or county governmental agency.

o Items not allowed:

- Fresh or dried meat or meat products including jerky, canned fruits (or) vegetables, flavored oils, salsas, etc, fish and shellfish products, canned pickled products (corn relish and pickles), raw seed sprouts, baked goods such as cream, custard or meringue pies and cakes or pastries with cream cheese icing or fillings, milk and dairy products including hard or soft cheeses and yogurt, cut fresh fruits and vegetables or juices made from these ingredients, ice and ice products, barbeque sauces, ketchups or mustards, focaccia-style breads with vegetables or cheeses.

- NOTE: It is best to check with your state and other regulatory agencies to ensure your great food product will qualify under your specific Cottage Food Act requirements. It is best to be compliant with agency requirements and have no unexpected surprises.

- **Commercial or Commissary Kitchens (licensed):**

  o Commercial or Commissary Kitchens have been inspected and licensed by the appropriate state (county and or city) regulatory agency and meet the requirements to produce items not allowed by the Cottage Food Act.

o These Commercial or Commissary Kitchens are equipped with commercial grade NSF equipment (such as stainless steel tables and sinks, large mixers, refrigeration units, and appropriate stoves, grills, and ovens, bottlers, etc.) Most of these kitchens will provide all the appropriate utensils, pots, pans, knives, etc. Most do not allow you to bring your own utensils into their licensed kitchens.

- NSF means National Safety Foundation. NSF develops public health standards and certifications that help protect food, water, consumer products and the environment. As an independent, accredited organization, NSF tests, audits and certifies products and systems as well as provides education and risk management.

o The client (vendor) must provide their own ingredients they will use in the preparation of their finished goods.

o The vendor will also have to provide their own jars, bottles, etc. to contain the finished product. The commercial kitchen should be able to advise you where to purchase the appropriate container, as well as boxes and labels. If not, you can find such information on the internet.

o The vendor will then be responsible to clean the facilities to pristine conditions before they leave.

o Some kitchens will not be able to handle all food products because of limited equipment etc. Check with the kitchen you are interested in using.

o As a client of the licensed kitchen, you must comply with state and local training requirements (see above). Because you are using a licensed kitchen, you then are allowed to use the kitchen's license for the preparation of your food items.

▪ NOTE: Usually the state has very strict requirements regarding the information, size etc of the data that must be on your label. Check your state requirements and be compliant.

▪ There are also independent commercial organizations which will test your food product to determine the "shelf life" of your product as well as the nutrient value of the product. Most states will require some kind of

expiration date, such as "use by or good until
_____" and nutrient values. Your commercial
kitchen should be able to put you in contact
with such an entity.

o Make sure you receive proper training from the kitchen
operator regarding the utilization of kitchen
equipment, etc.

o By using a licensed kitchen, you can then sell your
product wholesale or to others for resale.

o You can find a Commercial or Commissary Kitchen in
your local area by searching the internet.

o Commercial or Commissary Kitchens work, generally,
as follows. However there will be differences in the
operating requirements of kitchens.

- Some kitchens will require a monthly
"membership" fee. Whether or not you use
the kitchen, you will be charged a set fee.
Actual usage will be based on an additional
"hourly" fee – which includes clean-up time.

• Hourly rates are different for different
times of the day or night. There are
premium hours which will cost more

than non-premium hours, such as 2:00 am. Check with your kitchen.

- Some kitchens will have automated combination locks for entry. You will be assigned a code, which will open the door and also "log you in:" This in turn will generate an invoice based on the hours you had previously scheduled. Other kitchens will just give you a key for entry.

- Some kitchens will have their monthly schedule on the internet. You go online and schedule when you want to use the kitchen. You will be able to see what time slots and days are available. In other kitchens, you will have to call in and schedule with a real live person.

- Some kitchens will have video monitoring of the kitchens.

- Some kitchens will also provide you with bulk storage space or refrigerated storage space at an extra monthly charge.

Note: In some "home rule" cities, the health departments that regulate Commercial Kitchens may adopt their own regulations for retail production. These requirements may not carry over well when you want to move up to wholesale production. Ask your state department of health on the recommendations of which home rule city regulations are compatible with the state wholesale requirements.


## QUESTIONS:

**Does your state have a Cottage Food Act law?**

_____


**Will you use the Cottage Food Act or use a Commercial or Commissary Kitchen?**

_____


**What Commercial or Commissary Kitchens are near you?**

_____

_____

_____

_____

# Topic 28

# DESIRE AND PASSION

Many people who visit Farmers Markets will think the vendor has an easy job, particularly if the vendor is sitting down. But they would be wrong. Running your own business can be a lot of work. If you really want to grow your business, then you have to have a desire for success and a passion for your product.

There is a great analogy regarding the typical American breakfast of bacon and eggs that pertains to Desire and Passion. You see, the chicken is "Dedicated" to providing flavorful eggs, but the pig is "Committed" to providing flavorful bacon. The dedicated chicken can say, "If you do not like today's egg, then you might like tomorrow's egg." Whereas the committed pig only has one chance to provide that flavorful bacon and he has to die to provide it.

If you really want to grow your business into a real entrepreneurial enterprise, then your attitude has to be like the pig – willing to put all your effort into achieving your objective. You will have to have the passion to be constantly planning, evaluating, implementing and modifying your strategy for growth, at the same time developing and testing new products and meeting and surpassing your customers' expectations. Now I know that this sounds like a daunting process. But if you really believe in your product and you want to move from selling your product in one or two Farmers Markets to having your product sold in stores across the country, then that is the price you will usually have to pay. You have to be willing to briskly step into the unknown sphere of risk. But remember, this risk can be significantly mitigated if you do a great job of research, planning and implementation. (Also see the topics on Business Plans and Incubators).

On the other hand, if you do not want to expend the energy for significant growth, there is nothing wrong with the attitude of the chicken in our breakfast menu. Remember, eggs taste great too. You can still have significant success if you "desire" it and are willing to work for it. But it still takes good strategies, just not the intensity of the pig group.

Whatever "barnyard" of opportunity you choose to grow your Farmers Market adventure, enjoy the process!

## COMMITMENT

**I will commit the necessary hours to make my Farmers Market business a success!**

---

**Your signature and date**

Topic 29

# INCUBATORS – FOR THE SERIOUS ENTREPRENEUR

Incubators are places that nurture, train, encourage, refine and motivate the entrepreneurial spirit of your business enterprise. Incubators are usually associated with local universities, colleges, or other government service providers. Contact local universities/colleges to locate an incubator near you. Certainly, check the internet for incubators in your area. If you want to expand your Farmers Market business beyond the local business environment and reach to state wide, regional or national distribution, seek out an incubator to discuss your business ideas.

There are several great reasons to utilize an incubator.

- You will be assigned an experienced mentor to help you face and overcome the challenges of entrepreneurship.

- You might be able to rent a booth space or lab space if you desire.

- You will associate with other entrepreneurs to learn from and teach each other.

- You will learn things "not to do" which can be just as important, or maybe even more important for a startup, as the "things to do".

- There might be presentations from various business leaders willing to share their lessons learned and their struggles and successes.

## QUESTIONS:

**Where are you going to look for incubators?**

_____

_____

**What questions are you going to ask?**

_____

_____

_____

# TOPIC 30

# THE ELIMINATION OF WASTE, OR CONTINUOUS IMPROVEMENT

I worked in the automobile industry for over 20 years for one of the (former) Big 3. It was a great career.

In the late 1950s and early 1960s, Japanese vehicle manufacturers, mainly Toyota and Nissan (then called Datsun) were manufacturing and selling inexpensive, cheap, and in most cases poor quality small cars in the US market. The Big 3 (GM, Ford, Chrysler) paid these foreign interlopers little heed. This proved to be a major error in communal judgment, which almost destroyed the Big 3. They went from having about 95% of the market in those days to less than 50% of the total USA new car market today.

Japan is a country of scarce natural resources, as well as space. Japan was then, almost 20 years after World War II, still suffering from the effects of the war.

However, the president of Toyota, was an innovative manufacturer. He improved his vehicle designs and quality. Equally important, he started to cut waste and streamlined his manufacturing processes. Toyota vehicles started surpassing their customer expectations. Toyota originally identified seven wastes:

1. Transportation
2. Unnecessary Inventory
3. Wasted Motion/Movement
4. Waiting
5. Over Processing
6. Over Production
7. Defects

Today, there are additional wastes to be concerned about, such as not properly utilizing the skills and talents of your employees, and inefficient computer systems and programs, etc.

The elimination of the above wastes and incorporation of concepts of Lean Manufacturing and Continuous Improvement are the basis of what has become internationally known as the Toyota Production System (TPS). As an indication of the success of TPS and its impact on Toyota, Toyota is now the largest automotive manufacturer in the world with 2014 sales of about $250 Billion. That is almost $5 billion a week in sales.

The Big 3 finally saw the light and started to incorporate aspects of TPS. It was a long and difficult process taking years to accomplish, with many missteps and false starts. But eventually they got their acts together and incorporated TPS (under various different names). Today, most of the Big 3 can rival the quality of Toyota.

Today, worldwide, there is not a serious manufacturer, processor, service provider or professional who does not utilize some aspects of

TPS. As an example, even dentists are concerned about "production". The dentist has to consider and plan how many patients he/she can see in X number of hours, and provide them with a high quality professional and personable experience. The dentist has to plan and strategize how he/she is going to get those potential patients through his/her door and into the dentists' chair as efficiently as possible.

Now what does all this automotive history have to do with entrepreneurship in your Farmers' Market business? The answer is everything.

Some Farmers' Market businesses will launch on a shoestring budget. Most will not be able to survive many wrong decisions. If major companies can be laid low financially, by generating excessive waste, losing sight of customer needs and competitors improvements; how would a small company survive? They won't survive. These concepts are particularly important for those of you who want to expand your operations to state wide, regional or national distribution, the real small scale entrepreneur.

The good thing is that small scale companies are much easier to change, identify wastes, identify customer needs, and initiate effective changes. **A small business MUST be constantly vigilant against unnecessary wastes and continually strive to improve their business model.**

**QUESTIONS:**

How are you going to monitor your business performance?

_____

_____

_____

_____

How will you incorporate continuous improvement in your business?

_____

_____

_____

_____

# Topic 31

## "No" Usually Means "Not Today"

If you want to take the next step in growing your business beyond your booth at the Farmers Market and see your product in stores, you are going to have to become a salesperson to the retailer you want to market your product. You will have to promote your product and get the retailer and his customers excited about it. Some entrepreneurs provide samples in the store for tasting. This provides an opportunity for the retailer to see the sales potential of the product and how it will be received by the customers.

Marketing or promotion of your product is one of the business practices you have to give some serious thought about <u>before</u> you make your first call. You have to identify the correct person to speak to and then determine how you are going to get an appointment. What are you going to tell that person? This can be a very educational process – and fun! I suggest you do some role playing. I know that sounds hokey, but it really works. Another thing that leads to greater success, is to think BIG. Visualize your products on the store shelves in the next state, region or nationally.

For a small, local retailer (a local chain store), all you might have to do is stop in the store and talk to the store manager. If that is the case, you still have to be prepared.

When first starting, after every call, both on the phone or in a personal meeting, sit down and evaluate how things went – in writing. What were your strengths during the call/visit? What went right and why? What went wrong and why? Before you make that call or step through the door, you should already have planned (and practiced – role played) what points you want to make and how you are going to accomplish it. You should also anticipate what objections the buyer will raise and be prepared to provide answers that will alleviate those objections and hopefully turn them into strengths.

In a small one or two person company, the owner is almost always the salesman (at least initially). So in this situation, if you have had negative opinions about salespeople, get rid of those notions! The future of your company (on a local, regional, state or national arena) depends upon you making sales -- lots of sales.

Undoubtedly, however well you have planned and strategized, you are going to hear the word "no." As a salesperson, I don't like the word "no" relative to my solicitation of a potential customer purchasing my product or service. To me, the word "no" only means "not today." First it is extremely important to understand why the potential customer said no and then determine a strategy to address his/her objections.

Secondly, circumstances can change on either side of the sales equation. Who am I (or you) as a salesperson to make your customers decision for him/her? When we do not call back or visit the potential customer again, we have in effect made our customers decision for him/her – and that decision is a resounding "no"! There are a myriad of things that could change to necessitate another contact with the potential customer. There could be a new buyer or operations manager; you could have changed the packaging, pricing, distribution system, or you could have a new product.

However, there does come a time when "no" really does mean "no". That means instead of contacting the customer, say every three months, you contact him/her annually.

To be a successful entrepreneur, you need an attitude that your prospective customer **needs your product or service**. That does not mean you have to be cocky or have a self-righteous attitude. But it does mean you are self-confident. Don't let "no" discourage your efforts. Learn from it and move forward.

## QUESTION:

**How are you going to overcome hearing the word 'no'?**

_____

_____

_____

# ABOUT THE AUTHOR

Bill English is most happy to be a husband, father and grandfather. In his business career, he has worked at one of the Big 3 automobile manufacturers as a Quality Control Engineer. He is a student of Lean Manufacturing as well as being a budding inventor. Additionally, Bill has owned and operated several businesses, including an International Sales Agency, Advertising Promotion, Dry Cleaning and Cleaning Services companies.

He enjoys traveling, both domestically and internationally, for business and recreation. He has been in every state of the union plus 20 countries.

Bill is a people person. He loves to meet people and find out who they are. He loves to help people, hence this book.

Bill has been happily married to Frances for over 30 years. They are the happy parents of six children and grandparents to 12 grandchildren. Bill and Frances live south of Denver Colorado.

This is Bill's first book and a second book is in the planning stage, tentatively entitled "Letters From Dad to His Grown Children," advice and council to all. Bill believes we as parents, will never be released from our responsibilities and privileges of being a Mom or a Dad.

Made in the USA
Las Vegas, NV
28 June 2022